Jura Regiæ Majestatis in Anglia

Jura Regiæ Majeſtatis in Anglia:

OR, THE

RIGHTS

OF THE

ENGLISH MONARCHY.

WITH

REFLECTIONS

On Mr. *HOADLY*'s Book,

ENTITULED,

A Defence of his SERMON.

In a LETTER to a Perſon of Quality.

LONDON:

Printed in the Year 1711.

SIR,

YOU are pleas'd to demand my Thoughts on Mr. *Hoadly*'s Book; and indeed no Difficulties can supersede an Obedience to your Commands. A *Work*, which at first View, I thought insuperable to one of my mean Endowments, but after a second Perusal, and more reserv'd Thoughts, I discover'd in it many Inconsistencies, it having not one solid Principle for its Foundation · But is in Opposition to all allow'd Principles; Against all Authority, both Sacred and Humane; The general Consent of the Great and Learned in all Ages; Nay, against the Law of Nature it self, as I hope to evince, when I come to answer his Arguments, for I long to be at *close Hugs* with him. All which consider'd, I thought it strange, that a Book so Unwarranted, both by the Laws of God and Man, should find so general an Acceptance in this Nation

Now, Sir, I must observe to you, that you have nothing besides this Gentleman's *Bare Assertion* for what he saith, not one Orthodox Writer, not one Canon of any General Council, not one Statute of this Kingdom, or Imperial Decree, founded on the Law of Nations, to support his *singular Assertions*. He quotes, indeed, Mr. *Hooker*, in a *Particular* almost *Foreign* to his *Cause*, or what at least will very little promote it, in reference to an Original Contract I have not (I confess) the Book by me,

 and

and 'tis a long time since I read it: He doth, I grant, discourse of an *Original Contract*, but then, as I remember, he saith, *That the People had divested themselves by it of that suppos'd* Original Right *in themselves, and so lodg'd it in the Sovereign Power, as they could not resume it* This therefore, I'm sure, will not any ways authorize Mr. *Hoadly*'s Doctrine of *Resistance* ——

'Tis strange we should have no Account deliver'd down, when and where this Contract was made, in a Point so important to Mankind, in order to have perpetuated its Memory, much more than that of *Magna Charta*, so celebrated at such a distance. But enough of this *any Notion* .

He quotes likewise Bp. *Bilson*, representing him as speaking doubtfully, *That he knew not but in some Cases there might be Grounds for Resistance.* And so there may be, for meer Self-defence and Preservation, supposing there were such a *Tyrant Prince* as was never yet known in any Christian Nation, (tho', by the-by, 'tis observable, he stretches things to such Suppositions of *Tyranny* as were never known, and 'tis presum'd will never be) that should send Powers of armed Men to cut his Subjects Throats, Self-defence and Preservation would be extorted from Reluctance and irresistible Strugglings of Nature

But the *Opposition* and *Resistance* condemn'd, is what is first hatch'd in *Privy Conspiracies*, and improv'd into *open and avow'd Hostilities*, to Dethrone their Lawful Sovereigns.——

But I can quote him a true Passage from Bp. *Bilson*, who saith, *When Kings command what is right, they are to be obey'd, when otherwise, to be endured, either Obedience to their Wills, or Submission to their Swords, is due by God's Law.*

I

I must by the way observe of this *Author*, that he is of an acute and sophistical Wit; an elegant Style in his Expressions, with Arguments so plausible; as they may easily ensnare such as are not of Judgment and Penetration to search them to the bottom. And so confident he is, as to endeavour to evade the most clear evident Propositions, and always so held.

Wou'd any Man, besides himself, have had the Confidence to affirm, That tho' I swear Allegiance to my Prince, his lawful Heirs and Successors, yet that Allegiance is due to the Parliament, in Conjunction with the King and the Kingdom, and the Sovereignty invested in them equally? I would ask him where the Kingship and Sovereignty lies, when there is no Parliament, and before the *Triennial Bill* was extorted from the Martyr'd King (though I suppose Mr *Hoadly* will not call him so) by that *Rebel-Parliament*? The King was not under Obligation of calling Parliaments We knew when the House of Commons first began, and on what Occasion And whether they assume to themselves a greater Power than they had at their first Institution, is a *Point* too nice for me to determine: Tho' Thoughts are free

I wou'd bring on this Gentleman to *Principles*: They are call'd by the King's Writ, and by Virtue thereof made a Parliament, and the Breath of his Mouth dissipates them into Nothing Doth the King invest them with Power to Oppose and Dethrone him? And how can what is Supreme, divest it self of its Essential Sovereignty, by a Creation of any Subordinate Jurisdiction?

I must, on second Thoughts, return to the *Original Contract*, which the *Author* insists on, but on better Considerations (as I guess) fearing he might be be encounter'd with Arguments from that very *Topick*, he seems to decline it. *For*, says he, *in this* Original Contract *the People lodg'd no Power in the Prince to ruine them*; and so that *Contract*, on such *Supposition*, becomes void.

And may not the People of this Kingdom, on like Pretences, rise up in *Mutinies* against their Representatives in Parliament, for that they did not elect them to assess and lay on them such insupportable Burthens (as a discontented Party may, by Prejudice and Misinformation, be possess'd with?) No! they ought not, having debarr'd and foreclos'd themselves by their voluntary Choice, and intrusted them with an absolute and irrevocable Disposal of their Rights. For, were that revocable, they might then sit in Judgment on their Judges, against the very Streams of Natural Equity, and the govern'd Part (as my Lord of *Exon* observes) wou'd become the *Governing Part*.

It wou'd be too elaborate a Task for me, to follow the *Author* through all his Harangues and Particulars of Talk, but if in a short and succinct Method (which will be less tedious) I shall overthrow the main Foundations of that *Book*, and enervate those *Arguments*, which he so much triumphs in; I hope I shall then acquit my self to your Satisfaction, which is much the same Matter repeated over and over, and vary'd into new Flourishes of Words.

But one apparent *Fallacy* runs thro' the main Body of his *Book*. For he supposeth a Right and Power to *punish*, meerly from the *Delinquencies* of the Man, which is only the material or subjective Cause. The Right or virtual Power to punish, is in the Magistrate, and to him deriv'd down from the Supreme and Sovereign

Sovereign Power; and from whence there, but from the Almighty, who is *KING of KINGS and LORD of LORDS*? For unless we suppose some certain supreme and unaccountable Power, we give up the Cause to the *Presbyterians*.

For in this Particular, to observe the *Author's* Mistake, all the People collectively in this Kingdom can't punish the greatest Malefactor, tho' under the visible Guilt of any capital Crime. No! That Power lies only in the commission'd Magistrate, deriv'd down from the Sovereign Power; which overthrows the *main Fabrick* of his *Book*

He farther says, *The KING hath his Power from the Aggregate Body of the People.* Who told him so? Neither God or good Men ever so affirm'd. And 'tis ask'd him, How the People can transfer a Power they never had, *i. e.* A Power of Life and Death, since they have not Power over their own Lives?

To this he answers and affirms, *That they have*; and gives a Reason for it, (such as it is) *Because*, says he, *they venture and lose their Lives in Wars and Hostilities.* 'Tis true, they do so; but 'tis only by Force and Virtue of their Prince's Commission: They can't do it otherwise.

Thus you may see how easily his Arguments are silenc'd. The *Author's* grand *Assertion* is, *That there is lodg'd a Right and Power in the People to resist their Prince, for the Preservation of the Publick GOOD and HAPPINESS* (Which Words are the Burthen of the Song,) and so his Sovereign People are to be Judges of the Publick Good, (tho' fatally mistaken ones, the World never knew them otherwise.)

I would ask this Gentleman, by the way, What he means by the People? Whether the whole People? If so, then the Consent and Approbation of every individual Man must be had. Or whether he means the Richer, the Wiser, or the Stronger part of the People? Unto which side we shall turn to secure our selves? What if these People are divided among themselves (as it was never yet known otherwise) what shall we do? In what Manner and Method must we be commission'd to appear in Arms against our Sovereign? And on what Authority to act? And how must we proportion his Punishment in an equal Ballance with his Demerits, by any known Rule, unless the Clamours of a savage Multitude may be such? No Sir! All must sink into Anarchy and Confusion.

The fatal Consequences of this Doctrine are such, as the *Author* shall never extricate himself from by his *Fine Words*.

We know, that in that never to be forgotten *Rebellion*, a part of the People took up Arms against their lawful KING (a KING scarce to be parallel'd with a Prince of equal Merit and Clemency) on Pretence of Mr. *Hoadly*'s *Publick Good*, and another part of the People were of a different Opinion. And by the Ears they go.

Well! the Reforming Part (Mr *Hoadly*'s true Patriots) by Dint of Sword, gain the Power and Government, when long they had not sate, before another part of the People tumble them down, for a farther Advance of the Publick Good, and, in a short time after their *Usurpation*, another more godly and refin'd part of the People supplant them, for a more ample Improvement of the Publick Good. So at at length, they crumble into Confusion (as all things must which are propagated from Mr *Hoadly*'s Principles) Principles did I say? He hath not one For he opposeth all the most illustrious and convincing Authorities, both Divine and Humane, and makes the People Judges whether the Prince acts for the *Publick Good*, or not. You may observe how shuffling his Answer is to this Objection, tho' I shall force him to this Concession, That if there be such a Power independently in the People, Of punishing their Prince, if he acts contrary to the *Publick Good*, they must, by Consequence, be Judges of that Power, nay, and of the Extent of that Power.

I would ask this Gentleman, Whether he ever knew things to succeed well, when Inferiors reform'd Superiors; or when the People held the Reins of Government? No, Sir! The lamentable Massacres, prophane Sacrileges, and all the Enormities which *Lucifer*, with his Rebel-Angels, could have propagated on Earth, have been the sad Consequences in this, and all other Nations, where this Principle hath taken footing. It had almost laid wast the *German* Territories, begun by a Doctrine preach'd up by one *John Huss*, That the Emperor living in mortal Sin, might be depos'd: The Contagion spread so fast, as it reach'd almost the Palace Gates, making him so uneasy, that a Council was call'd at *Constance*, to prevent the further Evil. How nigh of Kin this is to Mr *Hoadly*'s plausible Doctrine, I leave you to judge. I dare say, he can hardly distinguish them, though so good as he is in making Distinctions where there is no Difference.

I will, by the way, submit this to your Consideration, Whether greater Evils have not always flow'd from the Government of the Populace, than

 from

from tyrannous Princes? I dare say, a long Succession of such, would not have drawn on this Kingdom such multiply'd Calamities as our late Civil Wars did, on Pretences and Protestations for the *Publick Good.*

The Author again says, *That all Obligations of Duty and Submission cease on the Subject's Part, when the Prince answers not the End of his Institution* (being the *Publick Good*) and the SOVEREIGN MOB must be Judge of that: So we have the *Good Old Cause* reviv'd, *That is,* says he, *when they are a Terror to evil Works, and not to the good* So indeed they ought to be, but on Supposition they are not so, who shall punish them, having no Superior but God? Unto which he replies, *That Censuring and Punishing are no relative Acts of Superiority.* As to which I observe, I believe he is the first Man that hath affirmed such a Solœcism with so much Confidence. He might as well have justified, not only a Disobedience in Children to Parents, but a Power in censuring and punishing them, being no Acts of Superiority, or, as if where there is lodg'd a Right and Power of Judging and Punishing, there was not imply'd a Power of Superiority over the judg'd and punish'd. Thus he makes the Bar to over-rule the Bench And in a like preposterous way of reasoning, he is pleas'd to say. That *when Kings exceed the Original of their Institution, they equal themselves with their Subjects.* So all along *the corrupted Blood of Forty One* runs in the Veins of his Book, separating the Person from the Office. I needed not to have hinted so much to a Person of Judgment. The very mention of these Doctrines carry a Confutation with them, (tho' I shall observe divers others before I leave him) and I can't forgive him his Reflection on King *Charles* the First, in his Answer to the Sixteenth

Objection

Objection mentioned in his Book; where, speaking of that excellent Prince, he hath this Expression,

Whatsoever Oppositions against him were necessary for the Publick Good, I think, ought to be defended.

Would any Man, but few Years since, have vented such a Blasphemy to that Prince's Memory, as if he had in his Reign so acted against the *Publick Good*, as to justify that unnatural War? No, Sir! He withstood not the *Publick Good*, unless his too great Condescention to humour his People, made it so, divesting himself of so many glittering Jewels of his Crown; I mean, so many essential Prerogatives to qualify a discontented People, wherein, if some particular Things were disputable, as the Ship-Money, Tunnage and Poundage, tho' aver'd by the Judges and greatest Lawyers at that Time to be within his Prerogative, his Majesty, for Satisfaction of his People, was pleas'd to disclaim them, and the People's Rights (if they were so) were secur'd to them (as my Lord *Clarendon* observes) and their Discontents allay'd, being first fomented and carry'd on by Men of Mr. *Hoadly*'s Sentiments.

For I appeal to Mankind, whether his whole Book be not a meer Incentive to Rebellion? And you may observe, when he argues for a Right in the People to oppose their Sovereign, 'tis advanced on Suppositions of such Barbarity and Usurpation of People's Rights and Personal Safeties, as no Christian Prince hath been ever yet stain'd with And yet the Man's Pen hath betray'd him, by opening his darkest Thoughts, in supposing such Miscarriages in that Prince, as might justify that Rebellion.

 From

From whence I enforce this on him, That if ſuppos'd Male-Adminiſtration in one of the beſt Princes that ever ſway'd the *Engliſh* Scepter, were a ſufficient Ground for War (as the Author inſinuates) it might conſequently juſtify a Defection from any Prince whatſoever, ſo you may gueſs at the Venom which lurks in the Man's Heart. 'Tis not ſo much the Failings of the Prince, either in his Perſon or Government (whatever the Pretences are) but Monarchy it ſelf he would have overturn'd.

But, bleſſed God! Could it be imagin'd, that any one, not under the Conduct of the Prince of Darkneſs and Sedition, ſhould at this time, and in this Kingdom, vent ſuch Doctrines, when our crying Sins are Pride and Diſobedience, as that the Laws of God and Man are ſcarce able to keep Men in a due Subordination to a Government, which they themſelves admit and allow of? And the Two great Virtues (which, if I may ſo ſpeak, do even adorn Chriſtianity) *Humility* and *Obedience*, are now more ridicul'd than practis'd, and the People incourag'd with plauſible Inſinuations to cheriſh thoſe Original Sins, and to riſe up in Contradiction againſt the Supreme Power, however rightful, (it matters not, if the People think otherwiſe) deſerves the ſevereſt Doom and Condemnation.

Alas! poor miſtaken Primitive Chriſtians, who ſuffer'd not under Chriſtian, but *Pagan* Emperors, in Conformity to the Precepts of their bleſſed Maſter, when they might, in all Probability, have reſcu'd themſelves by humane Force, and that on the very ſame Inducements, for the ſuppos'd Good and Happineſs. And what could be more ſo, than to propagate the Chriſtian Faith?

Nay,

Nay, that learned Doctor St *Paul*, who could certainly have us'd as forcible Arguments as any one, against the Tyrant-Power then in being; when the Blood of the martyr'd Christians water-ed the Streets, and the Cry of the Mob was *Christianos ad Leones*: At that very time how Emphatically he presses and advances the Doctrine of Obedience (not only for Wrath, but) for Conscience sake.

He well knew his Master's Doctrine, and that Sufferings and Martyrdom were to propagate it. But were these Primitive Christians discourag'd at this? No, For had they, the Christian Faith had whither'd in its first Blossom. But on the contrary, it grew so renown'd by their Sufferings, that the Grain of Mustard-seed grew into a Tree of that Dimension, that it overspread the Earth, the whole Empire and Emperor himself becoming Christian. They patiently submitted under the Divine Dispensation, until the Almighty, by a Miracle of Mercy, deliver'd them.

For the Imperial Army, like to perish through Extremity of Drought, and surrounded by the *German* Forces, implor'd their Deities, *Sed frustra*, saith the History, and in the last Extremity (*nam quid tentare nocebit?*) The Christians are order'd to their Prayers, and no sooner had they fall'n on their Knees, with Hands and Eyes lift up to Heaven, but the Heavens open'd, show'ring down Streams to refresh them. *Repente descendit jucundissimus imber* (saith a great Author), but Fire and Hail on their Enemies. And after this, in the Reign of *Constantine the Great*, when the Sign of the Cross, the Emblem of their Blessed Master's Sufferings, appearing on the Christian Banners, commission'd by a Voice from Heaven, *IN HOC SIGNO VINCES*, confirm'd their Faith, with the Conversion of their *Pagan* Enemies.

I might enlarge on this, but must return to the Author It is obvious, how weak his Answers are, (tho' beautified with all the Embellishments of Rhetorick) as to this Particular of the Primitive Christians urg'd on him in the Nineteenth Objection, mention'd in the Book, where he tells us, That *their Judgment in any difficult Point, ought no farther to be regarded, than it is founded on the Reason of the Thing, or the Declaration of Christ and his Apostles.* Very well Sir! But suppose we are at Variance one with another (as we are in this present Case) about the right Sense and true Meaning of these Divine Declarations, is not the Example and Directions of the Primitive Christians, who immediately succeeded the Apostles, and saw their Faith confirmed by their Practice, a good Guide for us? If you can shew me a better, pray do it. And that whereas *Tertullian* says, *They never came within Suspicion of Plots and Conspiracies* He answers, *They might not so, in order to gain Reputation with their Emperors* So we have again, only Suppositions instead of sound Proof; which stretch a long way thro' his Book, frequently begging the Question, or sculking in Generalities, to eclipse the Renown of these Primitive Heroes, attributing their Submission to politick Purposes, nay, to Craft and Hypocrisy.

And according to his Arguments, they must live in a State of Sin, he recommending it as a Duty, not only of Temporal, but Eternal Concernment, for Men by Force to rescue themselves from the Tyranny of such Kings as attempted their Ruin, and the Destruction of the *Publick Good*, &c. And then it might be so with these Christians, when their Cities and Camps were fill'd with arm'd Legions As *Tertullian* (not quoted by him in that Particular) observes: *When, could not they trust Providence*

Providence in so good a Cause, but tamely and sinfully submit to Heathenish Persecutions, suffering the Christian Faith to wither? (As must be inferr'd from him) tho' indeed, it flourish'd by it.

I am loath to mention any thing not material, but I can't pass by his instancing the *French* Refugees with the Primitive Christians, who, at this Day, disallow the sacred Order of Episcopacy. That those should be rang'd in the same Rank, and put in Competition with these Primitive Saints, is such a Piece of Confidence, as can only be match'd with a Chymical Presumption in extracting Rebellion out of the Thirteenth Chapter to the *Romans*; and by an unauthoriz'd Paraphrase, making St *Peter* and St. *Paul*, (as the Author does) Patrons of a Sovereignty in the People to sit in Judgment on, nay, in some Cases, to dethrone their Sovereign.

It is above my Pretence to attempt an Interpretation of these Divine and Mysterious Volumes; yet excuse me for saying, That on this Occasion, I have had recourse to some Libraries well furnish'd with Books in this way, and will offer him this, That if he can produce but one Commentator, either in the *Greek*, *Latin*, or *English* Church, that hath ever favour'd his Paraphrase, (but indeed the quite contrary) I will then ask him Pardon, which reflects on me an *Argumentum ad Hominem.*

Mr. Hoadly, saith one of a contrary Faith to him, *You have preach'd and written, that the Holy Scriptures are a plain Rule in all material Points, pray, how do you make this good, since so many profess'd and reverend Divines, and the Universal Church, according to your Arguments, have, Age after Age, been mistaken, both as to the Sense and Practice of these plain Scriptures, all of them living and dying in Error,*

that

till an illuminated Mr. Hoadly *(the World now drawing on to its last Period) has discovered to us the Truth?* How the Gentleman can extricate himself from this Difficulty, I know not. The Pretence he hath to St. *Paul's* Authority, is St *Paul's* Reasoning (as he calls it) for that *Kings are not a Terror to the Good, but to the Evil.* Though the Apostle tells us, *That those who resist, shall receive to themselves Damnation.* Thus would he make the Apostles Conclusion bear against his Premises.

But I beg leave to ask him this Question, Would not St. *Paul*, think you, have qualify'd the Difficulty in a few Words, by saying, *Unless the Publick Good and Happiness be in Hazard?* So when our Blessed Saviour so positively forbad Resistance of the Supreme Powers, and foresaw the black Clouds of Misery and Desolation hanging over his distressed and forlorn Followers; would he not (think you) have somewhat allay'd the Severity of this Doctrine (being so to Flesh and Blood) and have said, *But in case of a design'd Overthrow of your Good and Happiness, and your Ruin is attempted, then exert your selves, stand manfully to your Arms to resist and subdue such Tyranny as I never commission'd, for 'tis great and glorious?* (So are the Author's Words,) What can he say to this? Why, nothing at all, Sir, excepting his own false and singular Glosses on the Holy Bible, prophanely and impiously attributing to his Sense, the Dictates of the Blessed Spirit.

I thought, among the many Errors which have been impiously father'd on those sacred Records, that of Resistance to supreme Powers, could have the least Pretence, there having been no manner of Iniquity so much (as that) condemn'd, so quite contrary to the

the Ends of Christianity, and punish'd with the most exemplary Marks of Divine Vengeance, and that in case of Resistance to the worst of Kings.

Nebuchadnezzer, King of *Assyria*, wasted all *Palestine* with Fire and Sword, burnt the Temple, plunder'd away the Sacred Vessels, and led the People of *Judea* into Captivity; where he erected his Golden Image, and such as refus'd to worship it, he commanded to be cast into the fiery Furnace; and yet after all this, God Almighty calls him his Servant, and the Prophets *Jeremiah* and *Baruch* wrote to the *Jews* to pray for his Life and his Son's *Belteshazar*.

And the Prophet *Ezekiel*, in bitter Terms reproves the Disloyalty of *Zedechia* in revolting from him. The Case of *Saul* and *David* I need not instance to you. And the Prophet *Isaiah* calls *Cyrus*, tho' a prophane and wicked King, the Lord's Anointed.

I can't, by the way, but take notice of what hath been observ'd of our infallible Author, who having several times affirm'd, That *to pay Obedience to a King, acting against the Good of the People, as to the Minister of God, is Blasphemy. Because*, says he, *we make God Author of the Evil*; and being hardly prest with the Example of *Saul* and *David*, this unwary Expression drops from him very unlucky to himself, *viz*. That it had been the highest Crime in *David* to have kill'd a Man, whom he knew God had appointed to reign. What, had God appointed *Saul* to reign? And had he still the Divine Authority and Commission, when he had been guilty of so much Tyrany? And was he still the Minister and the Ordinance of God? Why else had it been so high a Crime in *David* to have kill'd him? Thus hath this renown'd Author made himself guilty of that Blasphemy he so rashly and unjustly charges others with. But we shall meet with more such Inconsistencies

In the New Testament, we find our Saviour *paying Tribute to Cæsar*, at the Expence of a Miracle, neither he or his Disciples inculcating any Dislike to the People in regard of his Religion

But I must do the Author Justice in this Point, who will not admit this Text to be of any Importance to his Cause, (for he is always his own Carver) especially in interpreting Scripture For, says he, *our Saviour's paying Tribute, is no Argument against lawful Resistance*, i e. *when the universal Good and Happiness is invaded.* Very well Sir! But you may please to remember, that in a few Pages before, you said, That *That when a King acts against the Ends of his Institution, which is the Common Good* (you have almost worn the Word threadbare) *he equals himself with the People, and so the Sovereignty sinks* Well then! I reply to you with this Dilemma. Did this Heathen Emperor, unto whom our Saviour *paid*, and commanding *Tribute to be paid*, rule by virtue of a Divine Institution or Permission, take which you please, or not?

Take which side you will, but pray speak out. If you answer me affirmatively, then neither you or your Book have said any thing to the purpose. If not, then you contradict both the Reason and Justice of our Saviour's *paying*, and commanding *Tribute to be paid*, because, when the Sovereignty is forfeited, the *Tribute*, which is only an Incident or Accession to that Sovereignty, becomes likewise forfeited I desire the Gentleman's Answer to this at his Leisure.

But notwithstanding his Subtilty and Learning, this is not the only indefensible Passage in his celebrated Piece; which I shall take further notice of, as I proceed,

I

I have more Instances to alledge from the New Testament. But, by the way, I form this Argument Whatever is a necessary Duty, both as to our temporal and eternal Happiness (as Mr. *Hoadly* in some Cases, makes Resistance of Supreme Sovereign Powers to be, is plainly reveal'd in Scripture, but Resistance of Supreme and Sovereign Powers, in any Case, is not reveal'd in Scripture Therefore Resistance of Supreme and Sovereign Powers, is not in any Case a necessary Duty. Or thus:

Whatever is prohibited in Scripture, is sinful, but Resistance of Sovereign Powers is expresly (without any Reservation) prohibited in Scripture.

Therefore Resistance of Supreme Powers is sinful · For this I take to be a Rule, That where any thing is literally and expresly prohibited, no particular Act relating to the Matter prohibited, can be warrantable, unless by a Dispensation as to that Particular, as clear and express as the general Precept is, *Fear God, Honour the King, touch not mine Anointed, think not evil of the King I have said, ye are Gods, where the Word of King is, there is Power, and who may say, What dost thou?* Is (I doubt with our Author) no canonical Scripture.

But there is one remarkable place in the 8th Chapter of *Hosea*, where the Almighty denouncing his Wrath and heavy Judgments, says *Israel hath cast off the thing that is good* And in the Verse immediately following, *They have set up Kings, but not by me, they have made Princes, and I knew it not.*

I think this knocks the main Argument in the Head, Of the People's making and unmaking Kings.

I remember, when I laſt waited on you, (pardon the Digreſſion) a Gentleman then in Company, having talk'd with no ſmall Confidence, of this ſuppos'd Power in the People, being full of *Republican Doctrines*, I ask'd him this Queſtion, *What Cauſe he could aſſign from any ſettled Principles, either Divine or Humane, for Forfeiture of the Crown? Yes*, he reply'd, *Leproſy is mention'd in Scripture as ſuch.*

Could he have ſaid any thing more againſt his Pretences, for if Leproſy was aſſign'd for ſuch a Cauſe, it muſt be the only Cauſe, and no other: For *Excepto firmat Regulam*; and if any beſides could have been, we muſt ſuppoſe God Almighty would have reveal'd it.

And from hence let me infer, That as Kings are accountable to God Almighty only, when they do amiſs; ſo, by his unaccountable Prerogative, he can doom them to Leproſy, or ſmite them with ſudden Death, and not permit Man, in a ſinful way, to do his Work, by a Violation of his ſacred Commands, to accompliſh his Divine Ends

Sir,

I am now to lay before you the Authorities of Humane Laws, and ſhall, before I come to a farther Anſwer to the Author's Arguments, and the better to clear the Way to it, make this Poſition; that the Kings and Queens of *England*, under God, claim their Crowns by Right of Conqueſt and Succeſſion; and ſtrange it is, that any *Engliſh* Man ſhould gain-ſay ſo evident a Truth, ſo apparent in our Statute Books; where we may obſerve, That all the Kings of *England*, down along to *Edward* VI. date their Acceſſions to the Crown from the Conqueſt, as we find the Statutes prefac'd,

and

and the Parliaments all along ſo recognizing; which I take to be a full Reſolution of that Doubt.

Now, that the King is abſolutely Supreme in his Dominions, and the Crown Hereditary, have been poſitive Doctrines, viſible in our Law-Books and Records, in all former Ages. Both *Bracton* and *Fleta* ſay, *So Hereditary, as that the King himſelf can't alter the Succeſſions, being independent on any Earthly Power: That the People, neither Collectively or Repreſentatively, have no Power over the Perſon of the King, and that the Laws are Directive, not Preceptive to him.*

Omnes ſub Rege, at Rex ſub nullo,
Niſi tantum Deo. Says *Bracton.*

Princeps non ſubjicitur Legi, ſays the *Civilians.* In Purſuance whereof, Sir *Walter Rawleigh* ſays, *Subjects are bound to fulfil the Law by Neceſſity of Compulſion, but the Prince only of his own Will and Regard of the Publick Good.*

I can't, by the way, but obſerve to thoſe Gentlemen who affirm, That Kings derive their Authority only from Human Laws; and yet theſe very Laws derive their Authority from the Kings: And had theſe Kings no diſtinct Authority beſide the Law of the Land, by what Authority did they make theſe Laws? And to give you an undeniable Authority, I mean, that great and good Man, Sir *Orlando Bridgman*, then Chief Juſtice, when he preſided in that moſt ſad and ſolemn Tribunal, as ever ſat on *Engliſh* Bench, *i. e.* in the Tryal of the *Regicides.* How does he, Day after Day, avouch the King's not being accountable to the People; being ſtyl'd (as he obſerves) in the Statutes,

Primo

Primo Jacobi Primi, the Lieutenant of God, as being immediately under God, and that he is Head of the Body Politick. *And then, I think*, says he, *'tis an undeniable Consequence that he is Supreme*, and then farther affirms, That *the Crown of* England *hath been ever owned, and in our Statute-Books, and in the Oaths of Allegiance and Supremacy, styl'd, the* Imperial Crown of England. *And what is an Imperial Crown?* says he, *Why, 'tis that, which as to the coercive part, is subject to none but God.*

Nay, look into the Statute *Primo Jacobi*, and you will find, the Recognition by that Parliament was, That the Crown was lawfully descended to the King and his Progeny.

And the Statute of the 13th of King *Charles* II. which one might think, should silence the Clamours of those Men, especially pretending so great a Veneration to Acts of Parliament, where the great and august Assembly, after the Miseries of a Civil War (which for the future to prevent) do recognize and acknowledge the King *to be Supreme, the Power of the Sword, and the Militia to be his Right, and that it is not lawful* (mark the Words) *on any Pretence whatsoever, to take up Arms against the King, or those commission'd by him.* What can Mr *Howell* say to this?

Then, for the Laws of the Church, I'll only refer you to *Alphonsus in Libro de Haeresi*, where he largely demonstrates, That the dethroning and taking up Arms against a lawful Prince, whatever the Colour or Pretence be, is denounc'd as sinful and heretical, which hath been so thought, and so fatally prov'd, in all Times and Places. 'Tis what brought the two Eunuchs in the *Persian* Court to their just Destruction, *Voluerunt insurgere*, saith

The Dethroning of King *Edward* the Second, is sometimes instanc'd, but of no more Force than the poysoning King *John*, or indeed, the murthering any lawful Prince. *De facto ad jus non valet consequentia.* We must live according to Precept, not Example. But,

These Mistakes arise through Ignorance of the *English* Monarchy, wherein I may affirm, That the same absolute Power which was in the Conquerour, is deriv'd down to her present Majesty. But, indeed, as the said Sir *Orlando Bridgman* hath observed, 'tis one thing to have an absolute Monarchy, and another thing to have the Government absolute without Laws, so it may be affirm'd, That her Majesty is every way as absolute a Monarch, as the Conquerour ever was, excepting such Liberties, Privileges, and Immunities, as have been given us by her Royal Predecessors. And,

This pray Note, That these Liberties and Rights we so much boast of, have been the free Concession and Grant of the Crown only, flowing to us from the Bounties of our Kings, (and think well we have requited them for it) and this is an unalterable Rule by the Law of *Nations*, That where the Liberties of a People, are not the Result of a natural Right, but flow to them, from the Condescention of the Sovereign Power; in such a Case, they can't claim any thing beyond the Words of express Grant, nothing by Inferences or parallel Cases. And if so, what becomes of our Author's Arguments?

And you may find this Grandeur and Supremacy of our Kings, by observing the Preface and Style of our first Statutes. *The King commands*, &c. and

faith the Text, and that was enough to attaint them. And so it was by the *Roman* Laws likewise, as *Tacitus* observes, *Qui deliberaverant, desciverant*; to hesitate and doubt in point of Allegiance, is Treason and Apostacy, and the first who spread the Contagion in this Kingdom, were the two *Spencers* in *Edward* the Second's Reign, which was afterwards, in two several Parliaments, declar'd *horrid Treason*

I grant, That in a Popular or Consular State, where, in the one, the People are the highest Empire, in the other the Nobility, tho' there is one as King: And in such like Governments, where the Prince hath not the Sovereign Right, he is liable to that Power which is greater than his.

Of the first, was the *Common-Wealth* of the *Lacedemonians*, which sometimes fin'd and imprison'd their Kings. And such were, in *Cæsar*'s time, the petty Kings of *France*

Of the other sort, were the *Roman* Emperors, at first oftentimes depos'd by the Senate But if the Sovereign Power be in the Prince, as it was in the three first Monarchies, and in the Kingdoms of *Judea* and *Israel*, and is at this time, in the Kingdoms of *England*, *France*, *Spain*, *Muscovy*, *Turky*, *Persia*, *Æthiopia*, &c. tho' the Prince may be an ill Man, yet neither ought his Power or his Person to be hurted.

For how can any Inferiour Magistrate (much less Mr *Hoadly*'s giddy Multitude) by way of Judgment, have Authority over their Prince, from whom all Authority is deriv'd, and whose only Presence doth silence and suspend all Inferiour Jurisdictions?

The

and *the King prohibits*, &c. And so down to the Reign of *Edward the* First, when they are thus prefac'd, *The King, with the Consent of the Earls and Barons, ordaineth and establisheth*, &c.

Not a Word hitherto of the House of Commons, until *Edward* the Third, when 'tis added, *At the special Instance and Request of the Commons.* It may be observ'd, That tho' the Descent of the Crown hath been sometimes interupted and snatch't from the Royal Line; yet the Streams of Sovereignty have reverted into the proper Channal, and such as have diverted it, have been declar'd as Traytors, by Laws now in Being.

But I am now to return to the Author's further Argument In the Objections to his Doctrine, which he hath advanc'd. It is further ask'd him, Why his *Original Contract* had not been Printed, for the Benefit of Mankind? And where it is to be seen, if the Power of Princes be founded on that, and not on a Divine Commission?

These are plain *Questions*, deserving a plain *Answer*; which not being for his *Turn* to do, he wou'd extricate himself, by asking another *Question* not at all to the Purpose, *viz. When the* Original Commission *from Heaven*, says he, *is to be discover'd in Plain Characters, impowering Princes to Rule according to their Wills, in Opposition to the Publick Good* (as he before explains it) *raising themselves above Oppositions on any Account whatsoever, then the* Original Contract *may be produc'd.* And so puts us off from a solid *Answer*, to a *scoffing kind of Inference*; *And 'till then*, says he, *the Two Suppositions are on a Level.*

Is not this Excellent? That one *private Man* in Subjection, and that by his own Consent and Subscription, both to the Ecclesiastical and Civil Jurisdiction of this Kingdom, shou'd *Accuse* Both, only on his *own Authority* of Error, in a Point of so main a Concernment, and call for *Proof* on their side, against his own *False Accusation?* Than which, nothing can be more Absur'd For had he been well study'd in the Law of Nations, he wou'd then have known, that the *Onus Probandi* lies on the *Accuser*'s side. Both Church and State are in Immemorial Tenure and Possession of this Doctrine, and therefore evident Proofs are required from the *Accuser*; or from him, who attempts a Dispossession of this Tenure.

The Old Rule is,

Olim possideo, prior possideo.

In short, I presume the Divine Commission of Princes is in many Places asserted, both in Holy Writ, and in our *English* Laws: Whereas this *pretended Contract* is no where Recorded, nor are the least Footsteps of it to be seen in our Laws.

Indeed, as the Divine Commission is *Explain'd* by Mr. *Hoadley*, it is not capable of being prov'd; not capable, did I say? Sinful to attempt it: And I'll tell you why:

For he requires Proof of GOD ALMIGHTY's Commissioning Sin, and would have us produce an Original Commission from Heaven, in plain Characters (as he terms it) Authorizing Princes to Rule according to such Methods, as He Himself admits to be Sinful!

We

We don't deny, indeed, but that ſome Princes may, and have, abus'd their Commiſſion, by acting ſinfully in the Adminiſtration of their Government, and againſt the Will of God, who will undoubtedly call them to an Account for it. But the Queſtion is (in which the Author always ſhuffles) what Power, grounded on any Original Contract, the People have to puniſh and to reſiſt our KINGS? Or what Methods God hath reveal'd concerning Reſiſtance, when the Prince abuſes his Commiſſion?

It is farther objected to the Author, That no Government can be ſafe under his Doctrine, which naturally diſpoſes Men of turbulent and factious Spirits, to oppoſe their Governours, encouraging all publick Diſturbances, and all Revolutions whatever.

To this he anſwers, by transferring the Queſtion (as he uſually does) to ſave himſelf from the Hardſhip of a plain Anſwer, That *if it be true, that no Governours can be ſafe, if his Doctrine be taught; it muſt be as true, that no Nation can be ſafe, if the contrary be taught*: And ſo runs away in an Harangue of Words, importing not a tittle more than his bare Aſſertion, unneceſſary to tranſcribe.

But in ſhort, his Deſign is, to bring into compariſon (which they ſay are odious, I'm ſure in our Caſe they are) the Miſchiefs, more or leſs, which may ariſe from theſe two Opinions. To which I reply, That it may be very reaſonably ſuppos'd, that Princes aſſiſted by the wiſeſt and moſt ſelect Councils, and indeed, more intereſted in the *Publick Good*, than the greateſt Subject can be, and under a more immediate Conduct of a Supreme Providence, ſhould be the beſt Judges of what is moſt conducible to the *Publick*

Good No! he will not admit this, unless we suppose Princes to be as the Angels of God, tho' they are styl'd little less.

Well then! I would know on what Grounds we must submit to the Judgment and Sovereignty of his People (being not as the Angels of God,) a Qualification he expects from Princes. No! they are at such distance from such Perfections, that I dare challenge any Instance in the World, where the People grasp'd the Reins of Government, but endless Confusions follow'd · So the Author disputes not only against common Reason, but common Experience.

By the way, I'll give a slight Instance, if only for Diversion.

We lately saw Mr. *Hoadly*'s infallible Multitude assembled, and so, questionless, would the greater part of that City, and the whole Kingdom, had it not been for dread of an arm'd Power, and had they not been better taught by the Church than by Mr. *Hoadly*, in defence of Dr. *Sacheverell*'s Doctrine, and for Condemnation of his.

Thus we find the Man cast by his own Judges, as he would fain have them be, or his Book is erroneous, one of these two undoubtedly fall on him: And I hope such an Instance may bear a great Sway with him towards his Conversion, which I heartily wish.

Truly Sir, whether these judicious Moderators were in the Right or no, I am not to determine; but if so, I think it is the first time they have been so.

But this I must tell the Gentleman, that these celebrated Judges are, and have been, very variable and unfix'd.

It

It is within my Remembrance, that the main Body assembled, acted contrary to the Judgment of the late Tribunal; for then they were demolishing Churches, but now Meeting-Houses. Ungrateful Men to so kind a Patron! having taken so much Pains to lift them into the Seat of Judicature, and the first Decree they past, was for his Condemnation: Besides, this Gentleman on another Account is unfortunate, for I never heard, nor any other Man beside, I dare say, that either in *England*, or any other part of the World beside, where the People sate in the Seat of Justice, that they advanc'd to so high a Pitch of Reformation, or claim'd so large a Power and Jurisdiction to themselves, as Mr. *Hoadly* places in them. He makes them Judges, not only of their Prince's Conduct, but the whole Legislature, nay, of the very House of Commons, by whom chosen and represented. And if so, when they act against the *Common-Good*, what must be done? I would gladly know: Why, throw them out of the House, as *Oliver* and his Soldiers treated them.

Now, according to this Method, the Author puts the People against the Representatives of the People. And what shall we do under this Difficulty? It is beyond my Pretence to draw Schemes of Government, and, I believe, it may puzzle Mr. *Hoadly*'s Politicks what Course to take. We are now on a Level, and all Subjection to Authority extinguish'd.

For, How shall we qualify some to govern us? By Elections. But who hath Power to convene the People to do it? And supposing the People equally divided, how shall Peace and Property be preserv'd in the mean while? Which (as may well be suppos'd) will not be a little invaded, unless we imagine, that the People have arriv'd to a State of Innocency, by the Practice of Mr. *Hoadly's* Doctrines. These Things, Sir, are only fit for Ridicule.

But now to be more serious, and to return to the Author's Method, in taking a View of the opposite Doctrines.

The one, we find founded on the Decrees of Heaven, and Sanctions of Human Laws. The other, on the Result of a giddy Multitude.

The one, adorn'd with a Supreme Irresistable Power, to unite its several Parts in a due Subordination: The other relaxes and breaks all in sunder.

The one, adorn'd with the Blessing of Beauty, Peace and Order: The other deform'd, and rent into endless Divisions.

In a Word, an Obedience on the one side, is a Conformity to the Divine Will, the other a wilful Apostacy, And if in the Discharge of our Duty, we should fall under some Severities, we must patiently submit to them, as coming on us by the Permission of God, whose Ways are past finding out, and Judgments unsearchable, but ultimately terminated in our Good, either by our Temporal Sufferings, to attone the Divine Justice, or to free us from eternal Miseries, and to recompence our Resignation in the higher Regions of Bliss and Immortality.

While the other side, by a too daring Judgment on the measureless Abyss of Divine Providence, judges all things according to human Success, and takes its Measures from human Events, and from what only comes within their own Ken. But the Author proceeds in this part of his Answer, and argues thus;

If, says he, *it be admitted, that a Separation from a Church, imposing sinful Conditions in her Communion, be justifiable; why not as well in the State?*

Ay marry Sir! But who shall be Judge, whether these Conditions of Communion be sinful, either the Subjects or the Governours in this Church?

This is the main Question, which I find he is very shy in medling with, by his slight passing it by. Only this I can't but observe, That there never hath been, or ever shall be, either Schism in the Church, or Rebellion in the State, if this Gentleman could have his Way.

Another Objection to the Author is,

That an indispensable Obedience to our Kings is enjoyn'd in Holy Scripture, without Limitation, or Restriction. To which he Answers, *That a general Obedience is likewise commanded in Children to Parents; and yet, in Matters sinful, they are not to obey.* I reply, not actively, but if the Parent commands what is sinful, will that justify the Child in turning him out of House and Home; and by Parity of Reason, not the Subject in dethroning his Prince for commanding what is ill. For that is the Point before us, to which he saith little to the Purpose, (tho' in Elegant and Rhetorical Phrases, which have led Captive many unthinking Men) only propagating Doctrines contrary to our Saviour's Directions, *viz. That if we are persecuted in one City, to fly to another.*

It is further objected to the Author, *That Resistance and Oppression, even of Tyrants, destroy more Lives than the greatest and most oppressive Tyranny.* Which

I take to be an undeniable Truth; and am bold to say, That a Succession of several Tyrannous Princes, wou'd not have involv'd this Kingdom in so much Misery, as our late intestine Wars, when the People took up Arms to reform their Prince for the *Publick Good*. Unto this he answers, by a trivial evading the Matter, *That the more bitter Persecutions are, so much the better for Christians so delighted with the Doctrine of Non-resistance.* Is not this incomparable? That because Martyrdom is to be crown'd and recompenc'd in another World, therefore we are wilfully to run into it here.

The Persecutions of Princes are (God knows) sore Calamities on their Subjects, who are warranted by all Lawful Means, consistent with Christian Doctrines, to prevent and avoid them. But if that can't be done; *of two Evils, it is best to chuse the least*, better to suffer here, than eternally, by the Guilt of Practices, inconsistent with the Pattern left us of a Crucify'd Saviour.

If on the one side we suffer, 'tis in Conformity to the Divine Dispensations of Heaven, for Ends only known to the Almighty, above our Comprehension.

On the other side, our Sufferings are voluntary, and wilfully determin'd by our own Judgments, repugnant to divine Directions. That which follows, is nigh of kin to this, the Objection to the Author being, That the worst Princes are to be accounted as God's Judgments, and therefore patiently to be submitted to. *So*, says the Author, (very elegantly) *are Fevers, Plagues, Fires, Inundations*, &c.

This

THIS is extraordinary indeed: But if these are God's Judgments, he hath in his good Providence supply'd us with Means, by his Blessing, to cure and allay them: And the Remedy, on the other side, is by his Absolute Appointment. That is, by our Meekness and Resignation, the most acceptable Sacrifice we can offer.

ARE not those doughty Arguments, to advance a Book to such a Popular Esteem, as it hath almost put the Nation in a Flame?

IT is also farther objected, That the Supposition of a Prince's destroying the Happiness of his People, is absurd and impossible.

TO this our Author answers, That *such as know any thing of Human Nature, and the Corruptions of Mankind, can't think it an unaccountable thing, for Men to act contrary to their Duty.*

I reply;

YOU are very right, Sir! But why may not your celebrated Tribunal, the People, act contrary to their Duty (as, by *Dire Experience*, we have often seen?)

AN Error on the one side, is our Fault; on the other, 'tis our Misfortune (not our Crime); which in the end (if patiently born) will be amply recompenc'd.

IT is again objected, That the Government of the worst of *Tyrants*, is better than *Anarchy* and *Confusion*, and the *Violence* of a *Lawless Multitude*.

TO which the Author answers, *That there would be somewhat in the Objection, if there were no middle Condition between* Tyranny *and* Anarchy; *and impossible to oppose a Prince, without running into a Lawless Confusion.*

I reply,

AND would willingly know of the Author, ſome Inſtances of this middle happy Condition he ſpeaks of: No! 'Tis obſervable, he does not inſiſt on any Precedent or Inſtance, before the late Revolution; to which he has ſuch frequent Recourſe on all Occaſions, that I'm at a loſs to think, what Streights the Gentleman would have lain under, had he undertook the Cauſe before, without this his *ſingular Inſtance*. For he can produce no other thro' the Univerſe, wherein he ſo blackens that Unfortunate Prince; and miſrepreſents him to that Degree of Malice, that one would think, regards to Her preſent Majeſty, ſhould have aw'd him into Deference and Reſpect.

BUT to return;

IT is farther objected to him, That Miſery and Slavery are only Words to amuſe the Multitude: Why then ſhould the Pretence of them plead for the Lawfulneſs of Reſiſtance? I muſt interpoſe as to this Objection, and obſerve, That the Words of *Miſery* and *Slavery* are inculcated by the *Objector*, under a Suppoſition, not as if they could be, but that they are deſignedly made uſe of, as Bugbears to affrighten the People from their Allegiance. The Author anſwers to this Objection, by ſaying, That *the ſame may be ſaid as to Reſiſtance againſt Robbers, Cut-Throats, and Foreign Enemies, invading our Country*

IS not this ſtrange, that he ſhould bring in Reſiſtance of Supreme Powers, by the natural Subjects of theſe Powers, into the ſame Ballance with Reſiſtance of Cut-Throats and Foreign Enemies?

THE

THE one we are warranted in; and the other prohibited by the Laws of God, Man, and Nature.

AND then to little Purpose, the Author instanceth a KING invading our Country: For this KING is not a KING to us, but an Usurper and Invader; and we are bound by our Allegiance to oppose and repel him.

A farther Objection is, That the Crime of one Relation, doth not dissolve the Obligation of the other: And tho' a Prince should so far forget himself, as to act in contradiction to the Ends of his Office; yet his Subjects are not absolv'd from their Allegiance.

TO this universally acknowledg'd Truth, and as old as *Aristotle*, the Author answers, by asking this Question, *Whether God Almighty, in so many Words, hath declared this?*

I reply on him, and ask him, whether God hath ever declar'd the contrary? The Proof lying on him, who opposeth so generally a receiv'd Truth, on no Authority but his own Judgment.

AND then again he instances (repeating his own admir'd Observations) in the Case between Parents and Children; on Supposition, a Parent should attempt the Life of his Child, Resistance is justifiable in the Child.

I reply;

THE Child, by the Impulse of Nature and Self-Preservation, may ward the Blow, but not wrest the Weapon from his Father's Hands, to destroy him with it: For that is our present Case. Or will it follow, That an Act of Cruelty in the Father, forfeits his Paternal Authority? It is true, God hath not authoriz'd him to play the Tyrant: But will his unjustifiable Behaviour absolve the Children from the

Duties of Respect and Obedience? I think not: And then what becomes of his Argument?

IT is then objected, How, in any Case, it can be justifiable for Subjects to resist their Prince, since he is not accountable to them, having no Equal, much less Superiour, in his Kingdom? So plain a Truth, as, one might think, should be uncontestable.

LET us see how he answers it.

STATES *and* PRINCES, says he, *are not accountable one to the other, yet have a Right to defend themselves one against another's Invasion and Violence.*

YES, who doubts it? But what is this to our Question, which only concerns the Duty of Subjects to their own Princes, confirm'd by their natural Allegiance, and Laws of God and Man?

AND he transfers the Question (as is usual with him) between Princes themselves, in their several Districts and Territories, who stand on a Level independent of each other, and have a Right to defend themselves against any unjust Violation of one or the other's Rights, not as Subjects are under Obligations to their Princes. This is remote from the true State of the Case.

BUT what comes next, is as bad, if not worse. *A Robber*, says he, *properly speaking, is not accountable to the honest Man, whose Life and Fortune he attempts, yet the honest Man owes so much to himself, as to keep off the Rogue.*

I reply;

WHAT is this to our Purpose? Tho' I am not of the Author's Mind, but think that the Robber is accountable to the honest Man whom he robs.

BUT

BUT in this Case, a Resistance is warranted in the honest Man, by Divine and Human Authority. And so, in a preposterous way, he would bring into a Ballance, the Resistance of a Robber, with the Resistance of a Subject to his lawful Prince.

IS not this proper Stuff to fill up a Book with?

BUT now he comes on to his main Argument, That *where a Prince acts without a Commission, and it can be no part of his Commission to ruin the Happiness of his People, in such a Case, the Subject stands in equality with the Prince.*

THIS is the great Pillar of this specious Fabrick, the Weakness whereof I come to evince.

THAT is, That the acting without a Commission (as he supposes the Prince to do) and the acting contrary to that Commission, by abusing it by an ill Administration or Exercise of it, are of a different and distinct Nature.

AN Accusation against a Deputy of a Province (as a learned Person hath observ'd) to his EMPEROR or KING, for oppressing his People, is of no Effect, for having no Commission

GOD Almighty gives no Authority, 'tis true, to Princes for Oppressing the People, for that were to make Him the Author of Evil: No, they are commission'd to govern well, but on a Violation of their Trust, they having no Superiour on Earth, are accountable to God Almighty only; from whom they had their Commission, not from the People.

AND, I think, to assert, That a KING acting in his Royal State, tho' in some Instances not justifiable (as a learned Person hath observ'd) is no such formidable thing to affirm, that he acts by Divine Commission; because he acts by Virtue of it, tho' he abuses it.

I hope I'm warranted in what I say, from the Instances before given, of such KINGS recorded in the *Old Testament*, and yet during their *Exorbitances*, and a long Continuance of them, are notwithstanding styl'd by the Prophets, *The LORD's Anointed*, which Character cou'd not consist with a Forfeiture of their Commission.

I shall ask the *Author* this *Question*

IF Princes may be *resisted*, to prevent the Ruin of the Country? Why not a *Partial Ruin* of it? And if *Resistance* may be justify'd, for the immediate Preservation of the Publick Good? Why not for some considerable Advantage to it? And we may reason from the very Dictates of Natural Justice, that if a Prince may by his People be dethron'd, (whereunto his Murther hath always succeeded) for a great Crime, why not for lesser Crimes proportionably?

THE Author doth indeed say, That *the Prince is not to be resisted for his Personal Failings, not for one single Act of Unjust and Arbitrary Power.*

BUT then this Concession is grounded on a wrong Bottom: He is not to be resisted in such a Case: But Why? Not because he is the Minister of God; but because 'tis not for the Good of the Community in such a Case to do it: 'Tis not from any Obligation or Conformity to that unerring or fundamental Guide in Christianity,

Qua solus Dei est Ratio;
Sed qua solum Populi interest.

It is not because God Almighty requires it; but because the Interest of the People calls for it: And so, according to an Irreligious Method, inverts and exchanges

changes the Divine and Eternal Inducements into ſuch as are Temporary.

AFTER this, the Author aſſerts, That *to pay Obedience to a Prince, as the Miniſter of God, and recognizing him as ſuch, when he acts towards the Ruin of the Publick Good, is no leſs than Blaſphemy*, as he is pleas'd to ſay: His Inference being, That we thereby make God the Author of Evil.

AND I anſwer, That for the like Reaſon he may ſay, we make God the Author of Sin, becauſe we ſay he hath endow'd Man with Freedom of Will, and Liberty of Action, who abuſeth it by his Commiſſion of Iniquity.

THUS you ſee Sir, a few Words overthrow the Author's boaſted Arguments.

IT is farther objected to him,

THAT the Ruin of our Conſtitution, the Civil War, and Murther of KING *Charles* the Firſt, were owing to the Principles taught in Mr. *Hoadly*'s Sermon I farther add, Who knoweth not this to be true, that knoweth any thing?

TO this he anſwers, That *the Doctrine he teaches allows not of Oppoſition to any Prince, but ſuch as act againſt the End of their Inſtitution, and attempt the Ruin and Miſery of their People committed to their Charge. So that* (ſaith he) *to ſay that his Doctrine juſtifyeth that KING's Enemies, is to ſay and inſinuate, that he was a Tyrant, and an Oppreſſor.*

BUT is not this a Wicked Inſinuation, that in ſaying an apparent Truth, which is, That the Author's Arguments do tend to the juſtifying that KING's Enemies, is to reflect Tyranny and Oppreſſion on him? Though 'tis well known, that his Enemies made uſe of the Author's very Arguments at laſt;

last; for at first, they did not soar so high. It was lawful in the beginning with them, to take up Defensive Arms only, for the *Publick Good*; and so from one degree of Wickedness to another.

FOR there is a certain Progress in Evil, and ascent by Steps (as an ingenious Man said) e're they arrive to the Consummation of Villany, as at length they did, declaring for the very Destruction of the KING, for that the Ruin of the Kingdom was attempted by him. Of which Matter of Fact, the People of *England* (as they called it) were made Judges.

NOW if this be not exactly Mr. *Hoadly*'s Doctrine, let God and Good Men judge.

HOW easily may ill Men imbibe this Poyson? Why, say they, if we may take up Arms to rescue ourselves from a final Destruction, Why not for some apparent Good and Advantage of the Community? For Rebellion, like the Sin of Witchcraft, multiplies one Iniquity upon another.

THE Commission of one Crime, induceth the Necessity of one more; from Pride to Disobedience, and from thence to open Force.

THUS we see in a long Chain of Wickedness, Men are many times reconcil'd unto what they at first abhorr'd.

SOME of such, who, in *Forty One*, were a kind of *modest Rebels*; in *Forty Eight*, sat with impudent Faces, in the enormous Tribunal. So 'tis in vain for a *Rebel* to circumscribe himself, or set Bounds to his Iniquity.

I am sure, the Author gives no small Encouragement for a Good Beginning, or rather a Revival of *the good Old-Cause*, and particularly from a Passage, I have before mention'd in his Reflexion on that *Martyr'd KING*, insinuating a Necessity of that *Rebellion*.

THE

THE *Author* hath the Confidence to affirm, That *the People are the proper Judges of the PUBLICK GOOD, and when their Ruin is attempted, of the Necessity and Measures of Defence.*

AND indeed, who can be properly Judges, according to his Way, but the People; since the Community (as he grants) consists of two Parts, the Governing, and the Governed? Now by all the Implications thro' his *Book*, the Governing Party are the suppos'd Criminals, and they only Accus'd and Arraign'd; And by whom, but his Unspotted Multitude?

FOR, I observe, we have not one unkind Word dropt of them: And who can possibly be the Judges, according to this Gentleman's Principles, besides themselves?

The *Author* saith farther,

THAT the People being left to their own Judgments, if they act amiss, the Fault is theirs, and they are to answer for it.

Is not this precious Doctrine?

'TIS from this *corrupted Fountain*, these *bitter Streams*, the very Source from whence our Calamities have flown: The Peoples *Clamouring*, allowed for *Liberty of Judgment*; *Liberty of Conscience*; and so immersing themselves in *Libertinism*, and all manner of *Enormities*, meerly from the *Dictates* of their *erroneous* and *misinform'd Judgments.*

BUT the Question at the last Day will be, Whether these People have taken the proper Methods, for a regular Information of their Consciences, from (such as are to direct them) the *Pastors* and *Teachers* for edifying the Body of Christ, *&c.*

AND to what purpose hath God appointed those Judges, if not for the Instructions of the People? Or, can it be thought probable, they would steer safely without such a Guidance, solely in their own Judgments (as the *Author* supposes they would?)

IT would be too tedious to recite the many *Absurdities*, that are consequent to this *Author's Propositions*, (tho' so much valu'd as he is.)

WE say, that usually Old Proverbs are True; *Give the People an Inch, they'll take an Ell.*

IF *Resistance* may be allow'd in one Case, they will easily be induc'd to stretch it a point farther. Give but a little Vent to the bounded Waters, and a Torrent quickly comes on; an irresistable violent Irruption overwhelms all. Within this Age, we have seen and felt the desperate Conclusions that have seconded such Premises

AND the very Inducements of our *Author's plausible Arguments* for the *Publick Good*, for the *Right* of *Community*, have beguil'd many Thousands, dying under the *desperate Guilt of Rebellion*, impenitently, with brandish'd Arms against their Sovereign, and against his very Person in the Eye of the Sun, and against the Light of Heaven, into Darkness and cruel Habitations.

Chide me not, Sir, for an hasty Judgment,
For I have a sad Tale to tell, *viz.*

IN other Sins, *Ignorance*, though it may not totally excuse, yet it mitigates the Guilt; only, in the Sin of *Rebellion* it is not pleadable.

THE Army that march'd under *Absalom's* Banners, for the *Publick Good*, did it in the Simplicity of their Hearts; but that did not excuse them.

IT

IT is farther objected to the *Author*;

THAT Christianity condemns *Frauds*, *Perfidiousness* and *Breach of Trusts*; and *Resistance* can't be practis'd by Subjects, without the Guilt of these *Vices*; and therefore Christianity cannot allow of such *Resistances*.

AND in the following Objection it is said, That Christianity is a *Suffering Religion*, and a *Doctrine of the Cross*, and therefore cannot allow of *Resistance*. To these two Objections he thus answers (how pertinent to the Matter, I leave you to judge.)

THE same Arguments (says he) *will prove that Christianity cannot allow of Resistance to Foreign Enemies, or the greatest Usurper; and that it is unlawful to resist a* Robber *or a* Cut-Throat.

STRANGE to me it is, That so admir'd an *Author*, should shelter himself under such inconsequent Arguments. *Resistance*, on the one side being justifiable by the Impulse of Nature, *Self-Defence* and *Preservation*, secur'd by the Laws of God and Man; and the other expresly prohibited by both.

AND so the *Author* in his usual inimethodical way of Arguing, confounds a lawful, with an unlawful *Resistance*. And according to this Strain he proceeds.

Resistance (says he) *may be as well prohibited to a Foreign Enemy invading us.*

WHY, good Sir, a few Words answers this; *Resistance* in the Case stated by you, is lawful and allowed off; but what you say, is far remote from the Point in Contest.

THE *Author* argues to as little purpose, saying, *If Kingship be of Divine Right, How ought we then to oppose, and use a Violence to Foreign KINGS invading us?*

I reply;

SUCH a Foreign KING is no KING to us; this Power and Kingship being circumscrib'd within his own Territories, and he is resistible, as being an Enemy to our Native Prince, unto whom only we are bound in Allegiance.

THE *Author* father says, *If there may be Resistance in Matters of a Private Concern, why not in a Publick?*

I reply;

IN Matters of a Private Concern, the Laws secure and provide Remedies for us, but a Publick *Hostile Resistance* of our SOVEREIGN, they condemn, and in the same Chapter, the *Author* thus asserts,

IF (says he) *it be, as is sometimes urg'd, that* Resistance *tends to more Sufferings, and temporal Evils, than the contrary, and Christianity be a Suffering Religion, it must allow of* Resistance, *rather than condemn it.*

I reply;

THIS is Sophistical Stuff with a Witness. It is not the proper Method of Christianity to court *Martyrdom*, or wilfully to run into *Sufferings*. But to give a Solution to this Fallacy, in few Words, to the Shame of this Gentleman.

THAT is, because I am commanded to suffer, rather than to do Evil, therefore I must resist and do Evil, because I may suffer.

What will he say to this?

A farther Objection to the *Author* is; That the *Doctrine* of this *Sermon*, is contrary to the Doctrine of the Church, as contain'd in the *Homilies*.

Mr. *Hoadly*

Mr. *Hoadly* hath reserv'd this Objection till last, being conscious, I believe, of the Truth and Force of it · However, he summons all the *Arguments* he can to overturn this Objection (if it were possible) which attacks the *Integrity* of the *Author*, as well as the *Truth* of the *Doctrine* he advances.

First, HE in his *Defence* and *Vindication*, makes use of a *Weapon*, which was made by others, long before to his Hands; he says, *Tho' he did subscribe to the Article concerning the Homilies, yet by that Subscription, he did not intend a full Assent to every particular Passage, or every individual Word and Sentence in the* Homilies, *but to the Tenour of the Doctrine set forth in them*. But surely, this Distinction will not serve his Turn.

FOR, there is as great a Difference between the Doctrine of the *Homilies*, and that advanced by the *Author*, as there is between Light and Darkness. Alas! What Pity 'tis, that the Compilers of the *Homilies* should give a Man of Sense, and an elevated Reason, so great a Trouble. For this Man will not be convinc'd, that the *Homilies* against *Rebellion* condemn his *Doctrine*, tho' it is so clear and plain a Matter; and clear, I dare say, to every Man's Apprehension, besides his own; yet, must they be gain-said on no other Grounds, besides his own Guesses and Conjectures, which stretch along way thro' his *Book?*

THE *Homily*, he says, *intended not so*, which is another Contradiction.

AS if the Compilers of the *Homilies*, intended contrary to what they said; for, I am sure, Words can't be more express than they are, which his forc'd Glosses cannot invert. Then he instances from the Practice of the Nation at that time, in sending Armies abroad for the Relief of distressed Subjects.

I answer him;

THAT was an Act of the State, or Civil Power, not of the Church, for whosoever will examine the History of QUEEN *Elizabeth*, and the Memoirs of her Reign, will find, that she did not assist the *Hollanders*, *French* or *Scots* (as they were *Rebels* to their respective Princes) but as their Princes were either Secret or Open Enemies to her Majesty, and then no wonder, if the Clergy, as Dutiful Subjects, join'd with her, against the open Practices, or private Machination of the Courts either of *Spain*, *France*, or *Scotland*.

BESIDES, *A Facto ad jus non valet consequentia.* We are to live according to Precept, not to Example.

THEN the *Author* instances from the contrary Practice and Opinion, to the seeming Sense of the *Homilies*, of great Men of unsuspected Zeal for the Church. Which concludes nothing, unless they were infallible.

AND Mr *Hoadly* very well knows, to his great Trouble and Confusion, That these very Men that were zealous enough for the Revolution, do disown *Resistance*, with the greatest Abhorrence, upon any Pretence whatever, to this very Day; Witness the Archbishop of *York*, the Bishop of *Exon*, Dr. *Atterbury*, Dr *Sacheverel*, and many others.

THEN the *Author* further surmises, from the general Expressions in the *Homilies*, For unto Generalities he hath frequent Recourse, where they say (the *Homily* later) That the Compilers no more intended Absolute Passive, than Absolute Active Obedience; and that they chiefly design'd the *Doctrine* of *Non-Resistance*, in Respect of good Princes, or such as were only guilty of Personal Vices.

AS to which confident Assertion, I shall not only refer you to the Words of that *Homily*, so plain, as I think, no one of a free and unbiass'd Understanding can

can hesitate on, but must acknowledge, that it was the general Doctrine of the Church of *England*, demonstable from the multiply'd Books and Sermons from Year to Year, during the Reign of that Princess, when the *Homilies* and all were compil'd all along without any interruption, before our Civil Wars, maintaining the Doctrine of *Non-Resistance*; and granting there were a few Men that spoke otherwise, What is that to the Doctrine of the Church?

I must on this Occasion observe of the *Author*, that both in this and other parts of his *Book*, he leaves the Doctrine of Active and Passive Obedience undistinguish'd, representing the one as much our Duty as the other.

AS if passively to suffer for not doing Evil, and actually to do it, were not very remote

BUT now, says the Author, who is long in this part of his Defence (so much concerning him) *a difficult Question may be ask'd, Who shall be Judge of this Resistance?*

I answer, says he, *the Subjects themselves, who alone feel the Necessity of it.*

TO which is reply'd, That they are fallible, and easily to be impos'd on.

WHEREUNTO he answers, *That if the Persons who object this, will discover where the Seat of Infallibility is, no one shall be more rejoic'd than himself, on the Discovery.*

PITIFUL!

BECAUSE an Infallibility may no be demonstrable, therefore the People may be as competent Judges as their Superiors, and of the Actions of their Superiors.

THEN he comes on to some Instances, wherein the People are allow'd the Liberty of Judging, particularly

cularly of Doctrines deliver'd them from the Pulpit.

THO' I think in a Matter wherein they are not the best Judges, unless we must suppose them wiser than their Teachers.

BUT supposing it to be so, the Question will be, Whether they have such a Power of Judging, as to turn their Pastors and Teachers from their Church and Pulpit? For that is the Case before us.

THEN he instances farther in Elective Kingdoms, where the People are to judge of the Qualification of the Person who is to rule

BUT this is remote from the Case of hereditary Monarchies.

THO' in the Elective Kingdom, the elected KING becomes Sovereign and Supreme, unaccountable to the People, above their Reach and Resistance.

THEN, among other frivolous Objections, *The People are to judge*, says he, *who are the fittest Persons to represent and make Laws for them in Parliament.*

THEY have such a Right, 'tis granted? But from whence originally deriv'd, but from the Concession of their KINGS?

FROM whence I infer, That from the Grant of a Power only to judge in Matters properly within their Sphere, for the People to extend it so far, as to sit in Judgment on their Sovereign (granting them this limited Power) is absurd to argue

IT is affirm'd by great and learned Men, That the whole Legislative Authority in *England*, was once in the Crown, as well as the Property of all Lands, which at this Day are held of the Crown God made KINGS, and KINGS make Parliaments. The Lords and Commons are now part of the Constitution, but not the Fountain of Constitution The Lords are made by the KING, and were his great Counsellors long

long before the Commons were taken in: Which was not, as Dr. *Brady*, Keeper of the Records in the *Tower*, in his Introduction to the *Old English History*, says, before the 29th of *Henry* III.

THE Author proceeds (for this Question pinches him) saying, *The People are allow'd to judge, when to refuse their Active Obedience; and that it is impossible for Subjects to exercise Passive Obedience in such a manner as may be most acceptable to God, without such a Judgment.*

Unto which I reply;

THAT these Things, wherein we are to withdraw an Active, and consequently to exercise a Passive Obedience, are so expresly prohibited by Divine Laws, obvious to the meanest Capacity, that 'tis morally impossible for the greatest part of the People in this Kingdom (for so they must be, according to the Author's Grounds) under a Christian Education, and a Church instructing them in this Doctrine, should be utterly ignorant of so plain a Duty so much inculcated. For they are allow'd as rational Creatures, *Judicium discretivum*, in Matters properly within their Sphere, but not to super-intend their Princes

THUS Sir, I hope, I have given a full Answer to every particular Argument of the Author, throughout his Book (to which any Regard ought to be had) tho' multiply'd into various Flourishes of Words, as is generally observ'd, excepting his bold and unwarrantable Interpretations of Scripture, being above my low Sphere. 'Tho' I can't forbear saying, That his Glosses are so inconsistent, wrested to a new and different Sense from all Authorities, both ancient and modern (as may be discern'd by an ordinary Capacity.)

I ſhall aſſume to my ſelf, however, to hint this, that the Scriptures themſelves tell us, that they are not of private Interpretation: And I am ſure his is both private and ſingular.

WELL, Sir, I have almoſt done, only to obſerve the Author's final Reſolve at his leaving us; wherein I'm to treat him with ſome cloſe Reflexions.

THAT Reſiſtance, ſays he, *that is for the* Publick Good, *I commend*; *what is againſt the* Publick Good, *I condemn*.

BOLDLY ſpoken! A *Reſiſtance* then there muſt be (it ſeems) if the *Author* thinks it neceſſary for the *Publick Good*, tho' thought not ſo by others.

AND muſt there be a *Reſiſtance* againſt the Miniſter of God, the Ordinance of God the Earthly God, in a Cauſe which the *Author* thinks fit? (For ſo much his Words imply) Wherein, I hope, I may be excus'd, if I am ſomewhat ſevere on him in this Point.

WHEREIN I demand his *Anſwers* to theſe following *Queries*.

WHETHER he can inſtance me one *Rebel* yet in the World, who us'd not the ſame Cant?

WHETHER *Corah* and his Fellow-Rebels, did not preach and practice this very Doctrine the *Author* ſo much labours to have propogated; clamouring againſt Abuſes in Church and State; upbraiding with Inſolence their Superiors, being zealous (as they pretend) for the *Publick Good*?

I ask farther, how, according to the *Author*, there can be any ſuch Sin as Rebellion, becauſe there never was any Government withſtood, but on Pretence of Abuſes, and poſſibly none ſo clear as to be exempted from them.

WHE-

WHETHER, according to his Argument, there can be any ſuch Vertue or Chriſtian Duty, as *Paſſive Obedience?* For we are not to ſuffer (tho' for Conſcience ſake) as if he would bid Defiance to the Doctrine of that great Apoſtle.

NO, the *Publick Good* muſt ſwallow up the good Conſcience. Whatever the Sovereign Power commands, if we think it not conſiſtent with the *Publick Good*, muſt be withſtood.

NO Patience, no Reſignation, no Chriſtian Submiſſion to interpoſe. Farewel to thoſe melancholly Doctrines! Farewel, you Chriſtian Severities! Self-Denial, Meekneſs, and Mortification! Let us live great, let us defend our Rights and Privileges. *It is glorious* (the Author's own Words) *to do it.*

ACCORDING to this Method, the Chriſtian Faith, after our Saviour had left this World, and his martyr'd Apoſtles (were it not for the Doctrine I am now defending) would have wither'd away, without the Acquiſition of that Renown of patient Suffering, whereby it will be perpetuated to the End of the World.

TAKE up your Croſs and follow me, ſaith our Bleſſed Saviour: No, it muſt not be ſo now; 'tis the *Sword* and *Buckler:* Our Lives are indanger'd, our Liberties circumſcrib'd, our Properties invaded: *To your Arms, to your Tents*, O Iſrael!

WHAT Government can ſubſiſt, when it muſt truckle under the Controul and Correction of the People? Can you think the Bleſſed God of Order intended ſuch a Method, from whence ſo many Abſurdities naturally flow?

UNHAPPY Government! which, of all things, ought to be ſettled, muſt now be left in an unſettled Condition.

AND to reaſon the Matter a little farther, as to Obedience either *Active* or *Paſſive* to the higher Powers, which is enjoyn'd without any Limitation in *Holy Writ*; and Damnation denounc'd againſt *Reſiſtance*, without Exception in any Caſe.

NOW, if there could be any Reſerves of Qualification for the one, or Diſpenſations for the other, we muſt then (with Reverence be it ſaid) ſuppoſe thoſe Sacred Writings defective in a Matter of the higheſt Importance.

IT is a Maxim in our Laws, That a KING of *England* can do no Wrong; And how then can he be puniſh'd?

ACCORDING to the *Author*'s new Doctrine, there muſt be a Sovereignty plac'd over the Sovereign.

AS if St. *Peter* had directed our Obedience to the People, and not to the KING, as Supream.

ACCORDING to the Pattern our vertuous Author hath given us, it will be of Difficulty to define and explicate a Rebel, nay, to find out one: For what the Rebel doth, is for the Happineſs of the Community. His Intentions are rightly levell'd, and that, he thinks, ſanctifies his Actions. If he dies, he dies gloriouſly, as a true Patriot of his Country, if he gains his Point, the Succeſs juſtifies the Cauſe, and unrighteous Means with him, ſhall advance to a righteous End.

AND the World would be involv'd under no ſmall Difficulty, in the Diſtinctions of *Good* and *Evil*, according to Mr. *Hoadly*'s Meaſures.

SIR, I muſt ſubmit myſelf to your better Judgment; and if I have ſaid any thing (which I have diſpatch'd in as ſhort and ſuccinct a Method, as poſſibly

bly I could) to put ſome Check to this ſpreading Contagion, I ſhall think myſelf happy.

THE Poiſon is finely gilded, and to do the *Author* Right, I think ſo great an *Error* hath ſcarce been defended by more *Plauſible Arguments*.

I may confidently call it a great *Error*, being ſo repugnant to the Principles of Chriſtianity, which now muſt ceaſe to be a Doctrine of the Croſs, or a Suffering Religion; which when (as deſerves to be conſider'd) firſt propagated, and thoſe bleſſed Doctrines of Subjection and Obedience taught, there was not one Chriſtian Magiſtrate in the whole World.

IT tends to the Subverſion of Kingly Government, by its *Incentives* to *Rebellion*; for it poſſeſſes the People with the Notions of a *Power in themſelves*, which GOD never gave, nor the People cou'd never claim, by Virtue of any Natural or Divine Law.

IT diverts the Streams from their proper Fountains; it interrups the very Courſe and Order of all Legal and Divine, as well as Natural Hereditary Right.

THOSE of the Community, who are to live in Obedience and Subordination, who are to be guided and determin'd by thoſe Superiors, are now ſet in a *fair way* to judge and determine them.

PARDON me, Sir, at parting, if I preſent you with a ſecond View of the *Author*'s two paramont Arguments, tho' anſwer'd before, ſo much reſerv'd and valu'd by him for two Reaſons.

AS to the Miſchiefs that muſt neceſſarily ſucceed them, and from the *Author*'s Confidence that they are above the Power and Reach of an Anſwer, which are to this Effect,

THAT

THAT *a Prince acting without a Commission*, (and God can't give him a Commission to do ill) *and he doing ill in his Government, becomes out of Commission, and stands on a Level with the People.*

This is plausible and taking.

BUT the Fallacy lies here, he erroneously supposes, That an Abuse of a Commission, or an Abuse of a Power, or part of that Power, is a Forfeiture of the whole Power, and that to the People. (That's the Mistake.) Should this Doctrine take root in this, or any other Kingdom, the Consequences might be so dreadful, as I leave to such who have due Regards to her Majesty, or any other Christian Princes, rightly to consider.

THE *Author* appears beautify'd with the like artificial Paint, when he falsely infers, That in paying our Obedience to our Prince, as the Minister of God, and as the Ordinance of God, when he acts irregularly, and against the Ends of his Institution, is no less than Blasphemy, (he from thence concluding, That we make God the Author of Evil.)

Unto which I reply,

THAT he may with like Reason say, That 'tis Blasphemy to affirm Man to be created according to the Image of God, because he commits Iniquity.

IF it may be thought not so very pertinent in the *Author*, so often to repeat his darling Arguments; I hope, it will not be improper in me to baffle them with fresh Instances.

AND

AND now Sir, in all humble and due Submission, if any thing hath been said unbecoming the Defence of so good a Cause, I throw my self on your Candour; my Intentions being, I hope, rightly levell'd, and under the Conduct of your Example and Commands, will powerfully plead an Excuse in small Failings. I am,

SIR,

Your most Humbly Devoted Servant,

A. R.

Lightning Source UK Ltd.
Milton Keynes UK
UKHW022254240720
367142UK00009B/200

9 781379 728924